Archaeology and History of Santa Fe Country

Editor
RAYMOND V. INGERSOLL

Managing Editor
JONATHAN F. CALLENDER

Prepared for New Mexico Geological Society
Thirtieth Annual Field Conference
October 4-6, 1979

NEW MEXICO GEOLOGICAL SOCIETY
SPECIAL PUBLICATION NO. 8
1979

CONTENTS

Foreword	Raymond V. Ingersoll and Jonathan F. Callender	v
Publications of the New Mexico Geological Society		vi
The Prehistory of Santa Fe Country	Linda S. Cordell	1
Indian and Spanish Mining in the Galisteo and Hagan Basins	A. H. Warren and Robert H. Weber	7
The Cerrillos Mining Area	Albert H. Schroeder	13
The Battle of Glorieta Pass, 1862	H. L. James	17

COPYRIGHT © 1979 by the New Mexico Geological Society, Inc.

The articles in this Special Publication were prepared for presentation at the 30th annual field conference of the New Mexico Geological Society, held in Santa Fe country on October 4-6, 1979. No part of this publication may be reproduced, stored in a retrieval system, or transmitted, in any form or by any means, electronic, mechanical, photocopying, recording, or otherwise, without the prior written permission of the copyright owner.

FOREWORD

This volume is a companion to New Mexico Geological Society Guidebook 30 (Santa Fe Country), and is not meant to be a comprehensive summary of the archaeology and history of the Santa Fe area. Rather, it is a collection of four articles that were prepared in conjunction with the Society's fall field conference, and which provide the reader with insights to a small part of the human history of the area. This Special Publication is the Society's first product primarily dealing with topics other than geology. We think that both geologists and non-geologists will find the articles to be interesting and informative, and that this volume will be a suitable complement to Guidebook 30. We thank the authors for their interesting and timely contributions.

Raymond V. Ingersoll
Jonathan F. Callender

PUBLICATIONS OF THE NEW MEXICO GEOLOGICAL SOCIETY

FIELD CONFERENCE GUIDEBOOKS

1. **San Juan Basin** (New Mexico and Colorado), 1950, V. C. Kelley, E. C. Beaumont and C. Silver, eds., 152 p., 40 illus.
2. **San Juan Basin** (New Mexico and Arizona), 1951, C. T. Smith and C. Silver, eds., 163 p., 71 illus.
3. **Rio Grande Country** (central New Mexico), 1952, R. B. Johnson and C. B. Read, eds., 126 p., 50 illus.
4. **Southwestern New Mexico**, 1953, F. E. Kottlowski, ed., 153 p., 70 illus.
5. **Southeastern New Mexico**, 1954, T. F. Stipp, ed., 209 p., 76 illus.
6. **South-central New Mexico**, 1955, J. P. Fitzsimmons, ed., 193 p., 66 illus. Prepared in cooperation with the Roswell Geological Society
7. **Southeastern Sangre de Cristo Mountains** (New Mexico , 1956, A. Rosenzweig, ed., 151 p., 61 illus.
8. **Southwestern San Juan Mountains** (Colorado), 1957, F. E. Kottlowski and B. Baldwin, eds., 258 p., 110 illus.
9. **Black Mesa Basin** (northeastern Arizona), 1958, R. Y. Anderson and J. W. Harshbarger, eds., 205 p., 106 illus. Prepared in cooperation with the Arizona Geological Society
10. **West-central New Mexico**, 1959, J. E. Weir, Jr., and E.H. Baltz, eds., 162 p., 91 illus.
11. **Rio Chama Country** (northern New Mexico), 1960, E. C. Beaumont and C. B. Read, eds., 129 p., 35 illus.
12. **Albuquerque Country** (New Mexico), 1961, S. A. Northrop, ed., 199 p., 83 illus.
13. **Mogollon Rim Region** (east-central Arizona), 1962, R. H. Weber and H. W. Peirce, eds., 175 p., 77 illus. Prepared in cooperation with the Arizona Geological Society
14. **Socorro Region** (New Mexico), 1963, F. J. Kuellmer, ed., 204 p., 90 illus.
15. **Ruidoso Country** (New Mexico), 1964, S. R. Ash and L. V. Davis, eds., 195 p., 64 illus.
16. **Southwestern New Mexico II**, 1965, J. P. Fitzsimmons and C. L. Balk, eds., 244 p., 73 illus.
17. **Taos-Raton-Spanish Peaks Country** (New Mexico and Colorado), 1966, S. A. Northrop and C. B. Read, eds., 128 p., 40 illus.
18. **Defiance-Zuni-Mt. Taylor Region** (Arizona and New Mexico), 1967, F. D. Trauger, ed., 228 p., 98 illus.
19. **San Juan-San Miguel-La Plata Region** (New Mexico and Colorado), 1968, J. W. Shomaker, ed., 212 p., 95 illus.
20. **The Border Region** (Chihuahua, Mexico and the United States), 1969, D. A. Cordoba, S. A. Wengerd and J. W. Shomaker, eds., 228 p., 159 illus.
21. **Tyrone-Big Hatchet Mountains-Florida Mountains Region** (southwestern New Mexico), 1970, L. A. Woodward, ed., 176 p., 84 illus.
22. **San Luis Basin** (Colorado), 1971, H. L. James, ed., 340 p., 226 illus.
23. **East-central New Mexico**, 1972, V. C. Kelley and F. D. Trauger, eds., 236 p., 128 illus. Special Publication No. 4 included with purchase
24. **Monument Valley** (Arizona, Utah and New Mexico), 1973, H. L. James, ed., 232 p., 160 illus.
25. **Ghost Ranch** (central-Northern New Mexico), 1974, C. T. Siemers, L. A. Woodward and J. F. Callender, eds., 384 p., 273 illus.
26. **Las Cruces Country** (central-southern New Mexico), 1975, W. R. Seager, R. E. Clemons and J. F. Callender, eds., 376 p., 243 illus.
27. **Vermejo Park** (northeastern New Mexico), 1976, R. C. Ewing and B. S. Kues, eds., 303 p., 242 illus.
28. **San Juan Basin III** (northwestern New Mexico), 1977, J. E. Fassett and H. L. James, eds., 307 p., 267 illus.
29. **Land of Cochise** (southeastern Arizona), 1978, J. F. Callender, Jan Wilt, R. E. Clemons and H. L. James, eds., 372 p., 328 illus. Prepared in cooperation with the Arizona Geological Society
30. **Santa Fe Country** (New Mexico), 1979, R. V. Ingersoll, L. A. Woodward and H. L. James, eds., 310 p.
31. **Trans-Pecos Region** (west Texas), Available Fall 1980.

SPECIAL PUBLICATIONS

1. **Bibliography and index of the New Mexico Geological Society Guidebooks, 1950-63**; compiled by S. R. Ash, 31 p.
2. **History of New Mexico Geological Society, 1947-1968**; by S. A. Northrop, 78 p.
3. **The San Andres Limestone: a reservoir for oil and water**, 1969; F. E. Kottlowski and W. K. Summers, eds., 51 p., 35 illus.
4. **Subsurface geology of east-central New Mexico, 1972**; by R. W. Foster, R. M. Frentress and W. C. Riese, 22 p., 11 figs. (includes 8 isopach maps); included with Guidebook 23
5. **Cenozoic Volcanism in southwestern New Mexico, 1976**; W. E. Elston and S. A. Northrop, eds., 151 p., 119 illus.
6. **Tectonics And Mineral Resources of Southwestern North America, 1976**; L. A. Woodward and S. A. Northrop, eds., 218 p., 207 illus.
7. **Field Guide To Selected Cauldrons and Mining Districts of the Datil-Mogollon volcanic field, New Mexico, 1978**; Charles E. Chapin, W. E. Elston and H. L. James, eds., 149 p., 87 illus.
8. **Archaeology and History of Santa Fe Country, 1979**; R. V. Ingersoll and J. F. Callender, eds., 18 p.; included with Guidebook 30.

MAPS

a. **Geologic highway map of New Mexico** (in color, 23 x 29 in.), 1980, in preparation
b. **Geologic map of the Sierra Country Region, 1955**; compiled by V. C. Kelley; included with Guidebook 6
c. **Geologic map of the Albuquerque Country, 1961**; compiled by S. A. Northrop and A. Hill; included with Guidebook 12
d. **Tectonic map of the Ruidoso-Carrizozo Region, 1964**; by V. C. Kelley and T. B. Thompson; included with Guidebook 15
e. **Tectonic map of the Defiance-Zuni-Mt. Taylor Region, 1967**; by V. C. Kelley; included with Guidebook 18
f. **Tectonic map of the Rio Grande Region** (in color, 18 x 37 in.), 1975; compiled by L. A. Woodward and others; included with Guidebook 26
g. **Geological and geophysical map(s) of the Socorro Area** (in color, 24 x 38 in.), 1978; compiled by Charles E. Chapin and others; included with Special Publication 7

All publications are available by mail from the New Mexico Bureau of Mines and Mineral Resources, Socorro, NM 87801. Guidebooks and Special Publications are available over the counter at the New Mexico Bureau of Mines and Mineral Resources; the Department of Geology, University of New Mexico, Albuquerque; Holman's, Inc., 401 Wyoming Blvd., Albuquerque; Pebble Pups Rock Shop, Las Cruces; and Roswell Map and Blueprint Co., 125 East 3rd St., Roswell.

THE PREHISTORY OF SANTA FE COUNTRY

LINDA S. CORDELL
Department of Anthropology
University of New Mexico
Albuquerque, New Mexico 87131

HISTORY OF ARCHAEOLOGICAL RESEARCH

Before the late 1920s, archaeological work in the Santa Fe area was primarily exploratory in nature. Early scholars were concerned with describing the variety of ruins to be found and their general relationships to the modern Rio Grande Pueblos. Early investigations usually concentrated on the largest ruins or on areas where prehistoric remains are abundant. The pioneer prehistorians had traveled extensively in the Southwest, and as a result, brought a regional perspective to their work. Many of their studies have not been superseded in scope. Thus, Nelson's (1914) study of the Galisteo basin remains the most comprehensive guide to the ruins of that area, and Kidder's (1915, 1924) observations of the Pajarito Plateau, Santa Fe and Pecos vicinities remain models of systematic recording and judicious interpretation.

Beginning with Kidder's work, and continuing today, major research emphases have included establishing local chronologies and attempting to determine the tribal or linguistic affiliations of various peoples whose ruined villages are investigated. The application of tree-ring, radiocarbon and archaeomagnetic dating techniques has resulted in fairly precise chronologies. Reconstructions of the specific cultural affiliations generally have relied on interpretations of spatial distributions of architectural forms and of ceramic types (Ford and others, 1972). Most of these reconstructions are not convincing, because architecture and ceramic types may reflect function and/or trade and alliance networks rather than ethnic affiliation or language (Cordell and Plog, 1979).

Since the late 1960s, the range of research problems addressed has broadened to include defining patterned relationships among types of sites, configurations of land forms and distribution of natural resources. Paleoenvironmental reconstructions, derived from tree-ring and pollen analyses, are of considerable importance in current syntheses and interpretations. Nevertheless, archaeologists generally work within small areas and define sequences of events relevant to these. The Santa Fe country of this conference encompasses several cultural districts (Santa Fe, Taos and the Galisteo basin), and parts of others (Pajarito Plateau and Albuquerque). While these districts are meaningful units for many archaeological purposes (Wetherington, 1968), discussing each one separately obscures general patterns that are more important to a basic understanding of prehistoric adaptations as a whole. The following account therefore sacrifices local details in order to provide a general overview.

EARLY MOBILE ADAPTATIONS

The remains of terminal Pleistocene-early Holocene hunters and gatherers, referred to as Paleo-Indians, are not represented well in the Santa Fe area. The oldest Paleo-Indian artifacts are those of the Clovis or Llano tradition, characterized by fairly large, distinctive fluted projectile points that have been found in association with mammoth and other Pleistocene fauna. Excavated Clovis sites have been dated consistently by radiocarbon methods at about B.C. 9500 (Jennings, 1978). Clovis points have been recovered from the modern ground surface in several localities in north-central New Mexico, and one specimen was collected from the Rio Valdez Divide in the southern Sangre de Cristos. Other stone tools associated with this find are not related typologically to Clovis, and it generally is agreed that the Clovis point has been used and deposited by a later group of people (Wendorf, 1960; Wendorf and Miller, 1959).

Later Paleo-Indian remains comprise a number of distinctive artifact assemblages and projectile-point types (e.g., Folsom, Midland, Plainview, Agate Basin and Eden) that are associated with *Bison antiquus* or *Bison occidentalis* and other fauna, but not with mammoth. Radiocarbon dates from excavated localities manifest considerable overlap, and chronological ordering is often ambiguous (Cordell, 1978; Jennings, 1978). The only excavated later Paleo-Indian site in the vicinity of Santa Fe is R-6, near Sapello (Judge, in press). The site as yet has not been reported completely, but it apparently represents a quarry that was used by the manufacturers of Cody Complex tools (Eden and Scottsbluff points and the distinctive, triangular, "Cody knife").

In view of the abundance of Paleo-Indian sites elsewhere in New Mexico (Cordell, 1976; Judge, 1973), it may seem unusual that so few remains of this antiquity have come from the region around Santa Fe. Examination of the distribution of finds, however, indicates that all are from loci that have been subject to recent, severe erosion (Cordell, 1978). It appears that land surfaces of the appropriate antiquity have not been exposed near Santa Fe.

ARCHAIC FORAGERS AND THE INTRODUCTION OF CORN: B.C. 5500-A.D. 500

Although it has been tempting to attribute the decline of Paleo-Indian megafauna hunting to climatic dessication of the immediate post-Pleistocene, recent paleoclimatological studies make this explanation untenable (Bryson and others, 1970). Apparently, complex and poorly understood interactions among world-wide human population increase, minor climatic fluctuations, decreased climatic equitability, and changes in social organization and technology eventually lead to a subsistence shift to an increased reliance on wild plant foods and smaller game (Harris, 1977; Reed, 1977). The term Archaic is used throughout North America to refer to these broad-spectrum foraging cultures.

It has been argued that during the Archaic, the Southwest became a distinctive culture area for the first time (Irwin-Williams, 1967). That is, the particular foraging strategies adopted in the Southwest reflect adaptation to local topographic settings and food sources. In addition, artifact assemblages include specific types of projectile points, scrapers, knives and grinding stones that are not part of the Archaic pattern in other regions. Importantly, it was in the context of broad-spectrum foraging that southwestern peoples adopted corn, a plant originally domesticated in Mesoamerica but eventually of central cultural importance to the Pueblos (Dozier, 1970; Irwin-Williams, 1973; MacNeish, 1964). Considering the pivotal nature of the Archaic, very little about it is known. Several factors are relevant to the lack of information. Archaic sites are not highly visible today, because they are the remains of ephemeral camps. The sites also may be buried under more recent cultural deposits. Many of the tool types in use during the Archaic persisted into later times. In general, Archaic sites consist of surficial lithic scatters. Their assignment to the Archaic is based on recovery of distinctive projectile-point forms that are relatively large, implying the use of a lance rather than an arrow, but not as finely made as Paleo-Indian points (Irwin-Williams, 1973).

In the Santa Fe area, a few Archaic sites are known from White Rock Canyon, the Galisteo basin, from high elevations in the Sangre de Cristos, and possibly, from the basalt bluffs north of Taos (Biella and Chapman, 1977; Honea, 1969; Lang, 1977; Renaud, 1942; Wendorf and Miller, 1959). The material from Taos is problematical because it was described before Archaic remains were defined and dated, and seems to consist of temporally heterogeneous remains. Lang (1977, p. 15) suggests that early Archaic sites in the Galisteo basin reflect an annual round encompassing territory at different elevations. He proposes that this pattern may have been conditioned by hunters following the seasonal movements of deer.

Evidence of corn is important to defining the later Archaic. The oldest dated remains of maize in the Santa Fe area are from Ojala Cave, in lower Alamo Canyon within Bandelier National Monument (Traylor and others, 1977). Two radiocarbon dates (B.C. 650 ± 145 and B.C. 590 ± 75) were obtained from the cave level yielding corn and Archaic artifacts. These dates are considerably more recent than those obtained for corn elsewhere in New Mexico (Dick, 1965; Reinhart, 1968). Several factors may be responsible for this apparent lag. Corn is perishable, and prior to sedentism and the construction of storage facilities, is likely to be preserved only in dry cave deposits. No systematic exploration of cave sites has been undertaken in north-central New Mexico. More important would seem to be that, in comparison to other areas of the Southwest, Santa Fe country is relatively favorable for broad-spectrum foraging. The marked topographic relief and elevation differences insure both considerable diversity of wild foodstuffs and a longer ripening season for their harvest. As long as population densities remained low, cultivation of crops would not have been necessary.

Although corn was adopted eventually, it at first had few observable consequences for the archaeological record. People apparently incorporated the use of corn into their mobile life style. The tools used to process corn (grinding stones, roasting pits and hearths) were those that had been used to prepare other grasses. Until about A.D. 500, the use of corn appears to have been rather casual. There is no evidence of a commitment to farming.

EXPANSION OF THE HORTICULTURAL PATTERN: A.D. 500 to 1200

There is evidence, from scattered locations, of a greater dependence on domesticates during this period. The evidence consists of more permanent dwellings and storage structures, the use of ceramic containers, and a shift in the location of sites to areas where potentially productive agricultural land is available. These changes are not uniform throughout the Santa Fe area, nor is there any indication that they appeared in any one location and gradually spread elsewhere. Rather, the data suggest that groups living at relatively low elevations gradually became more committed to farming first. Eventually, sedentism replaced highly mobile adaptations in the mountains as well.

The dwellings characteristic of this period are simple pithouses with associated surface structures that presumably were used primarily for storage. Pithouses are generally round with central firepits. Standard features include four roof-support posts and a ventilator opening. Pithouse walls only occasionally are found lined with plaster. Pithouse depth correlates positively with elevation (Bullard, 1962), suggesting that heat retention and heat dissipation may have been important considerations in using this type of domicile. The energy expended in providing shelter was relatively great considering that the available technology included only wooden digging sticks, and that in some areas, such as Taos, pithouses were excavated to depths of three meters (Loose, 1974).

Surface structures accompanying pithouses were of adobe or *jacal* construction. Where extramural excavations have been carried out, work areas and hearths have been found (Biella and Chapman, 1977; Loose, 1974). Archaeologists generally have interpreted pithouses and associated storage rooms as indications of year-round sedentism (Glassow, 1972). However, studies are being conducted in east-central Arizona that are designed to test the possibility that the structures represent only seasonal occupations (Rice, 1979).

Ceramic assemblages found with the pithouse villages vary in time and from one subarea to another. At excavated sites in the Santa Fe River drainage near White Rock Canyon, painted ceramics include Red Mesa Black-on-white and Piedra Black-on-white that are typical of Puebloan ceramics found in the San Juan Basin and on the Colorado Plateau (Biella and Chapman, 1977; Honea, 1971). Some of the painted ceramics and the unpainted utility wares consist of brown wares that are common in the Mogollon Mountains and in the area south of Albuquerque. North of Santa Fe, at sites near Tesuque, the southern types comprise a smaller portion of the ceramic assemblage (Allen, 1973; McNutt, 1969). The ceramic tradition represented at sites near Taos has been considered conservative, because Taos Black-on-white, decorated with black mineral-based paint on a white slip, and a variety of gray cooking types dominated the ceramic inventory for a relatively long time, and trade wares are rare (Green, 1976; Loose, 1974; Wetherington, 1968).

One relatively large and quite different site that may date to this time period is LA 825 in the Tesuque valley. The site consisted of about twelve small house units, each with from ten to twenty rooms, both circular and rectangular kivas (ceremonial rooms), and one very large or "great" kiva (Stubbs and Stallings, 1953, p. 155). The architectural discontinuity manifest at this site has been interpreted as evidence of a migration into the area by peoples from the San Juan Basin (McNutt, 1969). Alternatively, the site may represent political expansion into the Rio Grande by San Juan groups who were involved in broad, inter-regional trade networks; or the site may represent a local ceremonial and redistributive center. At the time that most of the people in the Rio Grande valley and adjacent uplands were occupying pithouse villages, the large, famous, multistoried towns of Chaco Canyon and Mesa Verde were built. The Santa Fe area was one of several locations that were economically important to the San Juan Basin. For example, turquoise processed at Chaco Canyon probably came from the Cerrillos mines (Weigand and others, 1977). There is no evidence, however, that the Rio Grande was well-integrated politically into the larger and more complex systems.

SMALL VILLAGES AND VILLAGE AGGREGATION: 1200-1600

The beginning of this period is marked by three features. First, there is an increase in the number of village sites indicating an overall increase in population. Second, surface dwellings consisting of rectangular rooms arranged in small roomblocks replace pithouses in most localities. Third, ceramic assemblages include Santa Fe Black-on-white, which is a finely made type decorated with black carbon-based paint. Santa Fe Black-on-white greatly resembles ceramics that were made in Chaco Canyon. Excavated sites that date to the thirteenth century include TA-26 and the oldest part of Pot Creek Pueblo, both in the Arroyo Miranda drainage (Vickery, 1969; Wetherington, 1968); Pueblo Alamo, Agua Fria Schoolhouse Ruin, Chamisa Locita, Lamy, the older portions of Arroyo Hondo and Pecos pueblos, and Pindi Pueblo, all near Santa Fe (Allen, 1973; Kidder, 1924; Schwartz and Lang, 1972; Stubbs and Stallings, 1953); and Piedra Lumbre Pueblo, Pueblo Largo and the Waldo site in the Galisteo basin (Kayser and Ewing, 1971; Lang, 1977).

Most sites are located along small drainages with easy access to seeps, springs and good agricultural land. In some cases, extensive linear grids that retard runoff and soil erosion were built (Lang, 1977). Although some scholars have attributed the production of Santa Fe Black-on-white to migrants from Chaco Canyon, the architectural features of kivas show continuity with Rio Grande-style pithouses and not with the kivas of the San Juan Basin. Thus, kivas are circular with central firepits. They lack the high benches and pilasters characteristic of Chacoan kivas.

The numerous small sites, the physical settings in which they are located, and the soil- and water-control features are indicative of an increased dependence on cultivated crops. Agriculture is not completely reliable in any one location in the middle Rio Grande drainage, because there is often insufficient rainfall or an inadequate growing season and extreme variability in both precipitation and growing season from year to year. There is no firm evidence that canal irrigation was practiced in the Rio Grande valley in prehistoric times, but even if it were, short-term droughts and floods would have been as devastating as they are today. The widespread occurrence of ceramic types, such as Santa Fe Black-on-white and its derivatives, suggests a high degree of social interaction among the small villages. The maintenance of intervillage alliance networks would have been critical to the subsistence security of each village, because they provide means of sharing local surpluses (Cordell and Plog, 1979; Plog, 1977).

After about 1300 or 1325, there is evidence of another episode of population increase. Some of the increase ultimately may have derived from peoples who had abandoned the San Juan centers, and some of the increase was probably local (Wendorf and Reed, 1955). A common response to the stress induced by the population was the abandonment of many of the small villages, and aggregation of people at a few larger villages in relatively favorable environmental settings. Aggregation is an efficient method of expanding the size of the group that regularly shares resources and cooperates in subsistence tasks (Martin and Plog, 1973, p. 354).

In the Taos district, population aggregation occurred at Pot Creek Pueblo and possibly also at "Cornfield Taos" (Ellis and Brody, 1964). Architectural details suggest that Pot Creek may have been ancestral to modern Picuris Pueblo (Wetherington, 1968). "Cornfield Taos," the site of the old Taos Pueblo, is within the village boundaries of the modern pueblo. Large communities also developed at Pindi Pueblo, Arroyo Hondo and at Pecos Pueblo. Of these, only Pecos survived as a population center in the historic period.

Between about 1350 and 1475, large pueblos were founded in the Galisteo basin on Galisteo Creek and its tributaries. Among the more famous of these are San Cristobal, Piedra Lumbre Pueblo, Las Madres and San Marcos. Many of the large Galisteo pueblos were multi-storied with roomblocks massed about plaza areas. Elaborate retaining dams, reservoirs and field houses are associated with these ruins (Lang, 1977; Nelson, 1914). Schroeder and Matson (1965) provide descriptions of the Galisteo villages reported and chronicled by the Spaniards.

The construction of agricultural facilities, including dams and terraces, also is noted for White Rock Canyon (Biella and Chapman, 1977); however, large villages are on the broad mesa top above the right bank of the Rio Grande (Bandelier, 1892; Stein, 1976). During the Pueblo Revolt of 1680, the Cochiti and some of their allies from Santo Domingo, San Felipe, Taos, Picuris and San Marcos joined the Navaho and Apache in refugee communities on the Poterero Viejo. Old Cochiti (Kotyiti) was built as a refugee community. The site was burned during de Vargas' reconquest but again was used as a refuge in the abortive revolt of 1696 (Abbink and Stein, 1977).

The large, late prehistoric ruins of the Pajarito Plateau (including Tyounyi, Tsankawi, Tshirege, Otowi, Puyé and Navawi) also are associated with check dams and farming terraces. These sites are located at slightly lower elevations on the plateau than the earlier and smaller communities (Steen, 1977). Shrines and other sacred areas on the Pajarito Plateau still are visited by Pueblo peoples, and of course, Puyé is maintained by Santa Clara Pueblo as their ancestral village.

Although village aggregation and the construction of agricultural features indicate an investment in farming, a diversity of faunal remains found at the villages suggests the importance of hunting as well. Steen (1977) describes a variety of game traps located on the Pajarito Plateau. Finally, there is evidence from both the historic and prehistoric periods that trade was of considerable importance to the Rio Grande Pueblos. In historic times, Taos, Picuris and Pecos had active trade with Plains groups to the east. Agricultural produce was exchanged for buffalo hides and meat at the well known annual trade fairs held at Taos. The extent of the prehistoric trade pattern is reflected in the distribution of Rio Grande glaze wares. Between about 1300 and 1700, red-slipped, glaze-decorated ceramics were traded widely both within the Rio Grande among the Pueblos and to groups on the Plains. Petrographic analysis of temper used in these ceramics suggests localized production centers which changed over time (Shepard, 1942). On the basis of petrographic studies, Warren (1970) believes that the Cochiti area was a major trade center for glazes from about 1325 to 1400, that San Marcos and other Galisteo villages became production and trade centers from 1350 to 1475, and San Cristobal Pueblo from 1450 to 1680.

CONCLUSIONS

The modern Rio Grande Pueblos long have been considered appropriate analogs for the prehistoric communities in the Rio Grande area. The Rio Grande Pueblos are seen as culturally conservative in that they have maintained their ethnic and linguistic identities, their religious beliefs, and patterns of kinship and other forms of social interaction. In many of these ways, of course, the modern Pueblo peoples have continued the ways of their ancestors. On the other hand, the ethnographically known Pueblo cultures have been disrupted, because they have had to cope with massive incursions of outside groups: Athabaskan speakers (Navaho and Apache), Utes, Spaniards and Anglos. Some of the alternative strategies that are reflected in the archaeological record have not been available to Pueblo peoples for about 400 years.

Three strategies that seem to have been of particular importance, but that have been disrupted, are heavy dependence on hunting and gathering in addition to agriculture, strong inter-village alliance networks and trade, and the opportunity to abandon villages and migrate when faced with severe economic crises. During the historic period, not only did the presence of "outsiders" constrain migration and relocation, but the introduction of livestock destroyed most of the wild resources that would have been important in times of stress. What we see among the modern Pueblos is a remarkable adaptation considering that former options have been closed.

REFERENCES

Abbink, E. K. and Stein, J. R., 1977, An historical perspective on adaptive systems in the middle Rio Grande, *in* Biella, J. V. and Chapman, R. C., eds., Archaeological investigations in Cochiti reservoir, New Mexico, vol. 1, a survey of regional variability: University of New Mexico Office of Contract Archeology, Albuquerque, p. 151-172.

Allen, J. W., 1973, The Tsogue site highway salvage excavations near Tesuque Pueblo, New Mexico: Museum of New Mexico Laboratory of Anthropology Notes 73, 40 p.

Bandelier, A. F., 1892, Final report of investigations among the Indians of the southwestern United States, carried on mainly in the years from 1880-1885: Papers of the Archaeological Institute of America, series 4, p. 1-591.

Biella, J. V. and Chapman, R. C., 1977, Significance of cultural resources in Cochiti reservoir, *in* Biella, J. V. and Chapman, R. C., eds., Archaeological investigations in Cochiti reservoir, New Mexico, vol. 1, a survey of regional variability: University of New Mexico Office of Contract Archaeology, Albuquerque, p. 295-316.

Bryson, R. A., Baerreis, D. A. and Wendland, W. M., 1970, The character of late-glacial and post-glacial climatic changes, *in* Dort, W., Jr. and Jones, J. K., Pleistocene and Recent environments of the central Great Plains: University of Kansas Department of Geology Special Publication 3, p. 53-74.

Bullard, W. R., Jr., 1962, The Cerro Colorado site and pithouse architecture in the southwestern United States prior to A.D. 900: Papers of the Peabody Museum of Archaeology and Ethnology, Harvard University, v. 44, 205 p.

Cordell, L. S., 1976, The Folsom site in retrospect: New Mexico Geological Society Guidebook 27, p. 83-86.

―――, 1978, A cultural resources overview of the middle Rio Grande valley, New Mexico: U.S. Department of Agriculture Forest Service (Southwestern Region), Albuquerque, 330 p.

Cordell, L. S. and Plog, F., 1979, Escaping the confines of normative thought: a reevaluation of puebloan prehistory: American Antiquity, v. 44, p. 1-28.

Dick, H. W., 1965, Bat Cave: School of American Research Monograph 27, 114 p.

Dozier, E. P., 1970, The Pueblo Indians of North America: Holt, Reinhart and Winston, Inc., New York, 223 p.

Ellis, F. H. and Brody, J. J., 1964, Ceramic stratigraphy and tribal history at Taos Pueblo: American Antiquity, v. 29, p. 316-327.

Ford, R. I., Schroeder, A. H. and Peckham, S. L., 1972, Three perspectives on puebloan prehistory, *in* Ortiz, A. A., ed., New perspectives on the Pueblos: The University of New Mexico Press, Albuquerque, p. 22-40.

Glassow, M. A., 1972, Changes in the adaptations of the southwestern Basketmakers: a systems perspective, *in* Leone, M. P., ed., Contemporary archaeology: Southern Illinois University Press, Carbondale, p. 289-301.

Green, E. L., 1976, Valdez phase occupation near Taos, New Mexico: Southern Methodist University Fort Burgwin Research Center Publication 10, 102 p.

Harris, D. R., 1977, Alternative pathways toward agriculture, *in* Reed, C. R., ed., Origins of agriculture: Mouton Publishers, The Hague, p. 179-244.

Honea, K., 1969, The Rio Grande complex and the northern Plains: Plains Anthropologist, v. 14, p. 57-70.

―――, 1971, LA 272: the Dead Horse site, *in* Snow, D. H., ed., Excavations at Cochiti Dam, New Mexico 1964-1966 season, v. 1: LA 272, LA 9154, LA 34: Museum of New Mexico Laboratory of Anthropology, Santa Fe, p. 6-32.

Irwin-Williams, C., 1967, PICSOA: the elementary southwestern culture: American Antiquity, v. 32, p. 441-456.

―――, 1973, The Oshara tradition: origins of Anasazi culture: Eastern New Mexico University Contributions in Anthropology, v. 5, 29 p.

Jennings, J. D., 1978, Origins, *in* Jennings, J. D., ed., Ancient Native Americans: W. H. Freeman and Company, San Francisco, p. 1-42.

Judge, W. J., 1973, The PaleoIndian occupation of the central Rio Grande valley, New Mexico: The University of New Mexico Press, Albuquerque, 361 p.

―――, in press, Early Man: Plains and Southwest, an interpretative summary of the PaleoIndian occupation of the Plains and Southwest, *in* Sturtevant, W. C., ed., Handbook of North American Indians.

Kayser, D. W. and Ewing, G. H., 1971, Salvage archaeology in the Galisteo dam and reservoir area, New Mexico: Museum of New Mexico Laboratory of Anthropology, Santa Fe, 120 p.

Kidder, A. V., 1915, Pottery of the Pajarito Plateau and some adjacent regions in New Mexico: Memoir of the American Anthropological Association, v. 2, p. 407-462.

―――, 1924, An introduction to the study of southwestern archaeology, with a preliminary account of the excavations at Pecos: Papers of the Phillips Academy Southwestern Expedition, v. 1, 322 p.

Lang, R. W., 1977, Archaeological survey of the upper San Cristobal Arroyo drainage, Galisteo basin, Santa Fe County, New Mexico: School of American Research Contract Program, Santa Fe, 368 p.

Loose, A. A., 1974, Archaeological excavations near Arroyo Hondo, Carson National Forest: U.S. Department of Agriculture Forest Service (Southwestern Region) Archeological Report 4, 47 p.

MacNeish, R. S., 1964, Ancient Mesoamerican civilization: Science, v. 143, p. 531-537.

Martin, P. S. and Plog, F., 1973, The archaeology of Arizona, a study of the Southwest region: Doubleday/Natural History Press, Garden City, 423 p.

McNutt, C. H., 1969, Early puebloan occupation at Tesuque by-pass and in the upper Rio Grande valley: Anthropological Papers of the University of Michigan, v. 40, 133 p.

Nelson, N. C., 1914, Pueblo ruins of the Galisteo basin, New Mexico: Anthropological Papers of the American Museum of Natural History, v. 15, p. 1-24.

Plog, S., 1977, A multivariate approach to the explanation of ceramic design variation (Ph.D. thesis): University of Michigan, Ann Arbor, 192 p.

Reed, C. A., 1977, The origins of agriculture: prologue, *in* Reed, C. A., ed., Origins of agriculture: Mouton Publishers, The Hague, p. 9-22.

Reinhart, T. R., 1968, Late archaic cultures of the middle Rio Grande valley, New Mexico: a study of the process of culture change (Ph.D. thesis): The University of New Mexico, Albuquerque, 356 p.

Renaud, E. B., 1942, Reconnaissance work in the upper Rio Grande valley, Colorado and New Mexico: Denver University Department of Anthropology Archaeological Series, 3rd Paper, 68 p.

Rice, G. E., 1979, Modeling microenvironmental reduction: Paper read at 44th annual meeting, Society for American Archaeology, Vancouver.

Schroeder, A. H. and Matson, D. S., eds., 1965, A colony on the move: Gaspar Castaño de Sosa's Journal: School of American Research, Santa Fe, 169 p.

Schwartz, D. W. and Lang, R. W., 1972, Archaeological investigations at the Arroyo Hondo site third field report 1972: School of American Research, Santa Fe, 47 p.

Shepard, A. O., 1942, Rio Grande glaze paint ware: Carnegie Institute of Washington Contributions to American Anthropology and History 39, 80 p.

Steen, C. R., 1977, Pajarito Plateau archaeological survey and excavation: Los Alamos Scientific Laboratories, Los Alamos, 97 p.

Stein, J. R., 1976, An archaeological survey of the Tetilla Peak recreation area: University of New Mexico Office of Contract Archaeology, Albuquerque, 42 p.

Stubbs, S. A. and Stallings, W. S., Jr., 1953, The excavation of Pindi Pueblo, New Mexico: School of American Research and the Laboratory of Anthropology Monograph 18, 165 p.

Traylor, D. and others, 1977, Bandelier: excavations in the flood pool of Cochiti Lake, New Mexico (ms. on file): National Park Service Southwest Cultural Resource Center, Santa Fe, 528 p.

Vickery, L. D., 1969, Excavations at TA-26 a small pueblo site near Taos, New Mexico (M.A. thesis): Wichita State University, Wichita, 140 p.

Warren, A. H., 1970, Centers of manufacture and trade of Rio Grande glazes (ms. on file): Museum of New Mexico Laboratory of Anthropology, Santa Fe, 54 p.

Weigand, P. C., Harbottle, G. and Sayre, E. V., 1977, Turquoise sources and source analysis: Mesoamerica and the southwestern U.S.A., in Earle, T. K., and Ericson, J. E., eds., Exchange systems in prehistory: Academic Press, New York, p. 15-34.

Wendorf, F., 1960, The archaeology of northeastern New Mexico: El Palacio, v. 67, p. 55-65.

Wendorf, F. and Miller, J. P., 1959, Artifacts from high mountain sites in the Sangre de Cristo Range, New Mexico: El Palacio, v. 66, p. 37-52.

Wendorf, F. and Reed, E., 1955, An alternative reconstruction of northern Rio Grande prehistory: El Palacio, v. 62, p. 131-173.

Wetherington, R. K., 1968, Excavations at Pot Creek Pueblo: Southern Methodist University Fort Burgwin Research Center Report 6, 104 p.

Palace of the Governors, 1881. Ben Wittick, courtesy Museum of New Mexico.

INDIAN AND SPANISH MINING IN THE GALISTEO AND HAGAN BASINS

A. H. WARREN
1705 Foothill SW
Albuquerque, New Mexico 87105

and

ROBERT H. WEBER
New Mexico Bureau of Mines and Mineral Resources
Socorro, New Mexico 87801

INTRODUCTION

The Southwestern Indians rarely overlooked a mineral deposit that could be exploited for artifacts and pigments, but gathered and mined these resources for many thousands of years. When the Spanish explorers arrived in New Mexico during the middle and late 1500's, the Pueblo Indians took them to many of the mine localities, often in exchange for beads and other trade items the Spanish brought with them from Mexico.

The Spanish came to seek mines of gold and silver. The interest and determination of the Spanish prospector are embodied in the words of Coronado in a letter to Mendoza, dated August 3, 1540:

"As far as I can judge, it does not appear to me that there is any hope of getting gold or silver, but ... if there is any, we shall get our share of it, and it shall not escape us through any lack of diligence in the search ..." (Winship, 1896, p. 563).

Between 1598, when the Spanish first colonized New Mexico, and the Pueblo Revolt of 1680, there are no records of mine grants having been made, but there are several references to the Spanish exploring mines in the Cerrillos, the Placers and the Placitas districts. Zárata Salmerón, Franciscan friar and resident missionary at Jemez between A.D. 1621 and 1626, wrote enthusiastically of the mines of New Mexico:

"As far as saying that it is poor, I answer there has never been discovered in the world a land with more mines of every quality, good and bad, than in New Mexico; there are mines in the mountains of Socorro, in the Salt Beds, in the mountains of Puaray [Sandia Mountains], in Tunque [Placitas?], at the entrance, in the *sienega*, in San Marcos, in Galisteo, in Los Pozos, in the Picuries; in this pueblo there are garnet mines, in Zama, and in all the mountains of the Xemez ..." (Salmerón, 1966).

Many legends have grown up around the mining activities of the Pueblo Indians and the Spanish. Perhaps the most persistent has been the belief that the Indians had no underground mines. "As for aboriginal mining, it is a myth" (Bandelier, 1892, part II, p. 13). Ironically, this belief itself became a myth, for recent archaeological investigations during the past decade have shown that the Indian not only quarried turquoise but mined extensively underground for minerals.

Another myth relates to the "enslavement" of the Indian miner by the Spanish and its role in the Pueblo uprising in 1680. The Indians are purported to have filled up the mines following the revolt so that the Spanish could not find them again. There is no documentary or archaeological evidence that Pueblo Indians ever worked Spanish mines in New Mexico or that the filling of the mines was other than by backfilling and erosion (Schroeder, 1976, this volume). There remains, however, the possibility that Hispanicized Mexican Indians (*gente de razon*) were engaged in prospecting, mining and smelting activities during the 17th and 18th centuries.

Until 1970 or later, underground workings containing stone tools and Pueblo pottery were believed to be evidence of the use of Indian slave labor in Spanish mines, but major differences in both artifacts and mining technology provide evidence that the Pueblo Indian was the first prospector and miner in the Cerrillos district. Potsherds dating as early as A.D. 1325 have been found in underground lead mines. Many of these are decorated with lead-glaze paint, possibly produced from minerals from the same mines. Dozens of prehistoric lode mines have been recorded in the Cerrillos district and two of these have been excavated partially.

Search for prehistoric mines has been made in many other mining districts in New Mexico, and evidence for many has been found. Archaeological data also are providing information about early Spanish and American mining activities, for which written records commonly are lacking.

PUEBLO INDIAN MINERS OF CERRILLOS

In past centuries, the rugged and barren hills of the Cerrillos district did not attract permanent settling by the Pueblo Indians. San Marcos Pueblo (see Schroeder, this volume, fig. 1), the nearest large Indian village, was occupied between A.D. 1300 and 1680. Other smaller settlements and possibly some farmhouses were located along San Marcos Arroyo and Galisteo Creek. Although no Pueblo ruins have been found within the mining areas, evidence of prehistoric mining is widespread.

Archaeological remains associated with Puebloan mining activities in the Cerrillos district include turquoise quarries and tunnels, lead mines of unknown depth but considerable length along surface exposures of veins, cobbing and sorting workshops, campsites, hearths, and sherd and tool scatters. The Mina del Tiro vein has evidence of prehistoric workings along 550 m of its exposed surface. Although depths of the mines are unknown, extensive waste dumps associated with prehistoric artifacts have been noted in several localities along the vein (fig. 1) (Warren, 1975).

Prehistoric workings at the Bethsheba mine were excavated to a depth of 8 m by members of the Albuquerque Archaeological Society (Grigg and Sundt, 1975), with work still in progress at the mine site. Greater depths probably were reached by the Indian miners, judging from numerous accounts in the territorial press. In 1883, for instance, Messrs. Blonger and Whale broke through to an old tunnel while sinking a shaft at the Bottom Dollar mine in the Cerrillos district. Stone axes, hammers and chisels were found in the old work-

Figure 1. Stone tools and minerals found at lead mines in sec. 8, T14N, R8E. Top row: tool and galena crystals from U.S. Grant mine; grooved axe from Rob Roy shaft. Middle row: lapidary stone and galena at L. C. Cloury workings. Bottom: grooved axe and hammer from lead mine; grooved axe from Bonito turquoise pits, Cerrillos district.

ings at a depth of 34 m (Santa Fe New Mexican, April 21, 1883).

The lead ore mined by the Pueblo Indians undoubtedly was used by potters to make lead-glaze paint to decorate the pots made in the Rio Grande area from about A.D. 1300 to the early 1700's. Abraded specimens of lead ore have been found in archaeological excavations of prehistoric sites in the upper middle Rio Grande region (Warren, 1969). The first written account of Rio Grande glaze-paint pottery can be found in the narrative of the Coronado expedition of 1540-42 by Castañeda:

> "... they have earthenware glazed with antimony [galena] and jars of extraordinary labor and workmanship, which were worth seeing.... There were also many pots filled with shining metal, selected, with which they glazed." (Winship, 1896, p. 511).

Coronado did not learn the location of the mines of the Indians and returned to Mexico disappointed. But other Spanish expeditions returned in the 1580's and 1590's to discover the mines of the Pueblos. Following the settlement of New Mexico by the Spanish colonists in A.D. 1598, competition for the lead ores may have resulted, as it has been reported that the Spanish mined lead at Cerrillos for bullets for their guns [and possibly also for the silver content]. But the Pueblos may have continued to work the lead mines well into the early 1700's, for glaze-paint wares continued to be made into the early decades of the century.

Although archaeological data indicating prehistoric lead mines were not found until the early 1970's, the prehistoric turquoise mines of Cerrillos have been well known the world over for more than a century. Perhaps the most famous of all turquoise mines is Mount Chalchihuitl, but many other localities include Turquoise Hill, the O'Neal mines, the Bonito and the Firefly quarries, and the Mina del Tiro turquoise pits. Innumerable other pits and prospects have been found throughout the Cerrillos district. Many prehistoric mines have been disturbed or destroyed following renewed interest in turquoise mining in recent years when open-pit mining using heavy equipment was carried out in the Cerrillos and other mining districts in the Southwest. During the same period, many of the ancient turquoise mines have been located, mapped and recorded by archaeologists, although the task is incomplete.

In the Cerrillos district, prehistoric artifacts found at ancient workshop or trimming areas indicate that the Indians also were mining pigments such as limonite, hematite and malachite. An outcrop of yellow-brown jasperoid suitable for flaked stone tools also had been exploited. At the Bonito turquoise mines, green chert or jasperoid was utilized for making flaked tools.

The prehistoric mines can be recognized by the presence of stone axes, mauls, picks, hammerstones, anvils and lapidary stones. The favored material for mining tools was an unaltered monzonite, but occasionally an imported rock was used. Sandstone slabs were preferred for lapidary work in processing turquoise. Scoops or scrapers made from large potsherd fragments have been found at prehistoric lead mines, but their function is not known.

The age of a prehistoric mine may be determined by the presence of pottery fragments that have been dated elsewhere with tree-ring methods. The earliest pottery noted at Cerrillos is Lino Gray, which was made circa A.D. 650 to 800. Other pottery present included early Red Mesa black-on-white (A.D. 850-950), Santa Fe and Galisteo black-on-white (circa A.D. 1175 to 1300) and Rio Grande glaze-paint wares (A.D. 1325 to 1700+).

In contrast, artifacts from the Spanish mining period included plain wares, olive jar fragments, Tewa Polychrome, Glaze F sherds (A.D. 1650-1700+), Mexican redware sherds, and earthenware crucible fragments with lead(?)-glaze coatings. Slag, burned adobe, *comales* or flat stone slabs, small fragments of lead ore, bone and charcoal commonly were associated with the Spanish mine and smelter sites. Stone mining tools were absent, suggesting that iron tools may have been used.

THE TUERTO SMELTERS

Four 17th century smelter sites in the New Placers district near Golden, New Mexico, provide evidence of what may be the earliest lode mining for extraction of metals in the western United States. Potsherds associated with the smelters are from vessels of types produced during the middle to late 1600's and include Rio Grande glaze-paint pottery (Mera, 1940) and "Faint Striated" utility wares, which first were described at Pecos Pueblo (Kidder and Shepard, 1936). The pottery which is associated with ore fragments, slag, metal and burned adobe indicates that Spanish colonists were mining and smelting ore from the nearby San Pedro Mountains during the 17th century.

When the Spanish conquistadores first arrived in New Mexico during the 16th century, they visited many of the Indian mines. The Rodriguez-Chamuscada expedition of 1581 found mines of San Mateo [San Marcos Pueblo] about a league distance from the village. Two years later, the Espejo expedition also referred to the mineral deposits near San Marcos (Hammond and Rey, 1966). Again in 1593, Castaño de Soso announced the discovery of mines near that pueblo; he also went to visit the mines to the south, probably in the New Placers or Placitas district.

Following colonization of New Mexico by the Spanish in 1598, mining and smelting of ore was reported at the pueblo of El Tuerto, possibly on the western slopes of San Pedro Mountains (Schroeder, 1976). The location of El Tuerto is not known, but may have been along the present Arroyo Tuerto in the vicinity of Golden. Records of mining activities during the first 80 years of Spanish colonization are scant. Spanish mining laws were strict and most of the mining activities may have been carried out without official sanction and associated records. Archaeological data often provide the only record of mining activity during these early years of Spanish colonization.

Ceramics and Dating

Potsherds from the four different smelter areas varied slightly in place and time of manufacture. One area has stone alignments suggesting foundations of former buildings as well as debris from smelters (Tuerto site 1). Potsherds here date between A.D. 1650 and 1700; temper types indicate vessels were made mainly in the Galisteo basin pueblos of San Marcos and Galisteo, but vessels from Pecos Pueblo, Zia and other Keres villages were represented. Sherds from a Puname Polychrome vessel from the Bernalillo area and at least three bowls from the Tewa villages also were noted. Utility wares present were all from a type called "Faint Striated," a thin-walled, plain black ware with faint exterior striations. The majority of utility wares were tempered with mica schist.

A nearby smelter area (Tuerto site 2) with an abundance of slag and ore fragments had a similar ceramic assemblage with vessels from the Galisteo basin, Pecos, Cochiti and San Felipe. No sherds of utility ware were found in this area.

At one isolated smelter site (Tuerto site 3), sherds were mainly from glaze-paint wares made in the Keres villages of San Felipe and Cochiti, and date between A.D. 1630 and 1680. Sherds and lithic scatters are slightly upslope from the concentration of slag, ore fragments and burned adobe. Two discs of hammered lead found in this area suggest workshop activities. Utility-jar sherds were common at this locality; one sherd was encrusted with tiny drops of slag or glaze, suggesting proximity and contemporaneity with ore-smelting processes.

One other isolated smelter site (Tuerto site 4) yielded sherds from a single red bowl, probably a glaze-painted vessel from the Galisteo Pueblo.

The surface sherd assemblages differ from contemporary Puebloan and Spanish homesteads and missions in several ways. Sherds of Salinas Red, the undecorated wares common at 17th century Spanish sites, were lacking in the pottery assemblages. A predominance of decorated wares at all sites may have some functional significance, although the present sample is small. The presence of the thin-walled, micaceous utility wares, to the exclusion of the coarse-tempered, thicker-walled jars of contemporary Pueblo potters, may be of some interpretive importance. The miners of Tuerto no doubt obtained their decorated pottery from the Pueblo Indians, but the origin of the utility vessels is unknown.

Although nothing is known from the mine(s) from which the ore was obtained, the source area is indicated by the mineralogy of the ore. The earliest mention of a registered mine in the area is the San Miguel mine, about 60 to 63 km south of Santa Fe (Schroeder, 1976, p. 38), in A.D. 1710. A mine share in the Nuestra Senora de los Reyes Linares mine on the San Lazaro Mountain at El Tuerto was registered in A.D. 1714 to Miguel de Coca (Twitchell, 1914). Bell (1870, p. 135-140) reported visiting several old gold, auriferous copper and argentiferous galena lode mines in the New Placers district and Sandia Mountains, most of which had been stopped up by the Indians during the Pueblo Revolt. Raymond (1875, p. 328) also noted alleged discoveries of pre-Revolt mines on San Pedro Mountain. In 1839, gold was "discovered" at New Placers and Tuerto became the central mining camp of the district.

ORES AND SMELTER PRODUCTS

Fragments of ore, flux, slag and metal bullion from three of the smelter sites (1, 2 and 3) provide a substantial basis for interpreting the source of the ore, metals extracted and metallurgical processes used in their extraction.

Ore fragments consist of a suite of oxidized copper minerals (malachite, chrysocolla and minor azurite) in a gangue of limonite, garnet tactite, quartz, and sparse specularite and magnetite. Two fragments are composed of fine-grained granular adularia with disseminated malachite and blotches of black Mn-Cu silicate; another is arkose encrusted with malachite and limonite. Coarse lumps of barren magnetite and limonite probably were used as flux in smelting the more siliceous ores.

On the basis of mineral composition and fabric of the copper ores and iron-oxide flux at the smelter sites, it can be suggested with considerable confidence that the mines from which they were obtained were in the nearby San Pedro Mountains (for discussions of the geology, mineralogy, mining history and production see: Atkinson, 1961; Jones, 1904; Lindgren and others, 1910; Yung and McCaffery, 1903). The source deposits clearly were of contact-metasomatic origin, as shown by the garnet tactite gangue. Oxidized copper minerals and an appreciable fraction of the limonite were derived by weathering of chalcopyrite, as indicated by the texture of the limonite-malachite intergrowths and a residual core of chalcopyrite in one ore fragment. Limonite pseudomorphs reflect the presence of pyrite in the hypogene mineral assemblage, and specularite and magnetite are minor associates. The abundance of adularia in two ore fragments is noteworthy. This assemblage strongly points to the San Pedro Mountains contact-metasomatic deposits, and more specifically, to the San Pedro mine, the oxidized ores of which were compared visually with the smelter samples. Magnetite for flux could have been obtained from other deposits that are clustered around intrusive stocks.

The slags show considerable variation in character, ranging from dense to scoriaceous, and vitreous to crystalline. Poor separation of the metal bullion of some smelter charges left numerous prills of metal trapped in the slag, requiring breaking and sorting by hand. One section of Tuerto site 2 was strewn with small granules of slag that may reflect use of slag granulation by chilling with water to aid in freeing entrapped metal.

Inasmuch as only copper ores were recovered from each of the three sites, it was assumed that copper was the only metal of value sought by the miners and recovered at the smelters. A number of small, irregular lumps of metal that are clearly primary products of the smelting process, however, tell quite a different story, for they are composed of mixtures of variable proportions of copper and lead. In view of our failure to find any evidence of lead ores or concentrates at the smelter sites, the metallic lead content of the bullion is highly indicative of the use of litharge smelting techniques, as described in 16th Century European smelting practice by Agricola (1556, p. 353-411). Two small lumps of litharge found at site 3 reinforce this conclusion. A late 19th Century example of litharge smelting in Mexico has been described by Austin (1883-84). By adding litharge (crude lead oxides) to the smelter charge, metallic lead was reduced with the copper. Molten lead has a much greater affinity for the small amounts of silver and gold contained in the copper ore than does metallic copper, thus the precious metals tend to be extracted selectively into the lead fraction of the copper-lead bullion. Separation of the lead from copper was achieved in a subsequent operation that utilized the lower melting point of lead to liquify it and drain it away from the more refractory copper in a process known as liquation (Agricola, 1556, p. 519-521). In a third stage, the lead was melted on a hearth in a current of air, and selectively oxidized and vaporized by cupellation, leaving a residue of silver-gold alloy (Agricola, 1556, p. 464-483; Austin, 1883-84, p. 190-191). The condensed lead oxides from cupellation (litharge) could then be added to the next charge of copper ore in the primary smelting furnace, completing the cycle of the litharge process. The original source of the litharge is unknown, but it may have been from cupellation hearths treating argentiferous lead bullion in the Cerrillos or Sandia Mountains areas. The spongy copper residue from liquation was resmelted and refined in one or more stages, depending upon the quality required. It was then suitable for use in fabricating a wide variety of utilitarian and ornamental goods that were much in demand in the frontier region of 17th Century New Mexico.

In the absence of carefully controlled excavation of remains at the smelter sites, little can be said concerning the design of the smelting furnaces used there. Burned, bloated and fused adobe and smaller amounts of local stone with fused surfaces indicate use of these materials in their construction. It is inferred that small blast furnaces of adobe and stone using hand-operated bellows for draft were employed, rather than the more elaborate works portrayed by Agricola for the larger smelting complexes of Europe. Perhaps there was a similarity to the primitive smelters (*hornos*) of the Santa Eulalia district in Mexico, all too briefly described by Cleland (1921, p. 19), that were "18 in. wide at the top, 16 in. across the bottom, and stood nearly 4 ft. high." The charge for each smelt was "something more than 100 lb." The lack of sulfide in the ores of the Tuerto smelters obviated the production of a matte (metal sulfide melt), thus simplifying subsequent processes used to recover the contained metals.

CUCHILLA DE SAN FRANCISCO MINES

A group of prehistoric mines and quarries, apparently worked for malachite and azurite, is located along the Cuchilla de San Francisco in the Placitas mining district. The mine dumps are littered with stone hammers, grooved and notched axes, picks and flakes. Potsherds found in association with the mining debris are from Rio Grande glaze-paint vessels dating circa A.D. 1500 to 1550.

The mines are located on a narrow cuesta capped by massive resistant sandstone (Permian), which dips about 20° to the east. An adit about 12 m long was excavated beneath the sandstone cap along the dip slope, its ceiling heavily coated with soot (fig. 2). Two "gloryholes" and one quarry are located on the southern part of the ridge. Cobbing and sorting activities probably were carried out at the entrances to the workings, as mineral fragments, tools and pottery were found on the ground surface above the mine dumps. The large prehistoric pueblo of Tonque is about 3 km to the northeast, so that it is not surprising that most of the sparse sherds found at the mines apparently are from vessels made at that village.

Malachite and azurite have been used extensively by Southwestern Indians for ornaments, including pendants and beads, for fetishes and other carved objects, and for pigments (Ball, 1941). Bolton (1916) reported that the Pueblo Indians had many sources of these minerals, and that in 1598, a squad from Oñate's expedition to Arizona inspected a shaft three *estados* [ca. 5 m] in depth, from which the Indians extracted "brown, black, water colored, blue and green ores." In the Keres villages, White (1948) found that azurite and malachite were used much by the Keres to make a blue-green paint which is "applied to the bodies of male dancers, to leather arm bands, kachina masks, the ball of the Kástocó'ma . . . and to other articles of ceremonial paraphernalia." Dutton (1963) reported little turquoise at Kuaua, near Bernalillo, but a "notable amount of malachite."

SUMMARY

"From a historical standpoint, no section in the United States is possessed of so much interest." Fayette Jones, former and subsequent president of the New Mexico School of Mines, wrote these words in 1904 regarding the Cerrillos district.

Mining archaeology has long been a neglected field in the study of Southwestern history. W. H. Holmes (1919) of the Smithsonian Institution visited and described Indian mines and quarries throughout North America. Since then, only occasional investigations of prehistoric and early historic mining have been made. The mining districts of the Hagan and Galisteo basins are of particular importance due to their tri-cultural history.

The turquoise and lead mines of Cerrillos played a central role in the economy of the prehistoric Indians of the Rio Grande valley. The mines of the Tuerto as well as those of

Figure 2. Entrance to 12-m adit at Cuchilla de San Francisco prehistoric copper mines, Placitas district.

Cerrillos undoubtedly influenced early Spanish explorations and settlement of New Mexico and the daily lives of New Mexican citizens well into the 20th century. The American prospectors and miners of the late 19th and early 20th centuries were following well traveled paths as they staked their claims, pitched their tents and sank their mine shafts.

REFERENCES

Agricola, G., 1556, De re metallica, translated and annotated by Herbert C. and Lou H. Hoover, The Mining Magazine, London, 1912 (1950 reprint edition): Dover, New York, 638 p.

Atkinson, W. W., Jr., 1961, Geology of the San Pedro Mountains, Santa Fe County, New Mexico: New Mexico Bureau of Mines and Mineral Resources Bulletin 77, 50 p.

Austin, W. L., 1883-84, Smelting notes from Chihuahua, Mexico: American Institute of Mining and Metallurgical Engineers Transactions, v. 12, p. 185-192.

Ball, S. H., 1941, The mining of gems and ornamental stones by American Indians (Anthropological Papers 13): Bureau of American Ethnology Bulletin 128, 77 p.

Bandelier, A. F., 1892, Final report of investigations among the Indians of the southwestern United States, part II: Papers of the Archaeological Institute of America, American Series III and IV, Cambridge, part I, 319 p., part II, 591 p.

Bell, W. A., 1870, New tracks in North America, Scribner, Welford Co., New York (1965 facsimile reprint): Horn and Wallace Publishers, Albuquerque, 564 p.

Bolton, H. E., 1916, Spanish exploration in the Southwest, 1542-1706: Charles Scribner's Sons, New York, 487 p.

Cleland, R. G., 1921, The mining history of Mexico: a historical sketch, part I: Mining and Scientific Press, v. 123, p. 13-20.

Dutton, B. P., 1963, Sun father's way: the kiva murals of Kuaua: University of New Mexico Press, Albuquerque, 237 p.

Grigg, P. S. and Sundt, W. M., 1975, A progress report on the archaeological excavation of the Bethsheba mine: Albuquerque Archaeological Society, Albuquerque, 5 p.

Hammond, G. P. and Rey, A., 1966, The rediscovery of New Mexico, 1580-1594: Coronado Cuarto Centennial Publications, 1540-1940, volume III: University of New Mexico Press, Albuquerque, 341 p.

Holmes, W. H., 1919, Handbook of aboriginal American antiquities: part I: introductory: the lithic industries: Bureau of American Ethnology Bulletin 60, 380 p.

Jones, F. A., 1904, New Mexico mines and minerals, world's fair edition: New Mexican Printing Company, Santa Fe, 349 p.

Kidder, A. V. and Shepard, A. O., 1936, The pottery of Pecos, volume II: papers of the Phillips Academy southwestern expedition: Yale University Press, New Haven, 636 p.

Lindgren, W., Graton, L. C. and Gordon, C. H., 1910, The ore deposits of New Mexico: U.S. Geological Survey Professional Paper 68, p. 170-175.

Mera, H. P., 1940, Population changes in the Rio Grande glaze paint area: Laboratory of Anthropology Technical Series Bulletin 9, 41 p.

Raymond, R. W., 1875, Statistics of mines and mining west of the Rocky Mountains: U.S. Government Printing Office, Washington, p. 328.

Salmerón, Z., 1966, *Relación* (translated by Alicia R. Milich): Horn and Wallace Publishers, Albuquerque, 122 p.

Santa Fe New Mexican, April 21, 1883, Santa Fe.

Schroeder, A. H., 1976, A history of the area along the eastern line of the Santo Domingo Pueblo aboriginal title area: prepared for the U.S. Department of Justice, Santa Fe, 113 p.

Twitchell, R. E., 1914, The Spanish archives of New Mexico, v. 1: The Torch Press, Cedar Rapids, 525 p.

Warren, A. H., 1969, Tonque: one Pueblo's glazed pottery industry: El Palacio, v. 76, p. 36-42.

─────, 1975, An archaeological survey of the Occidental Minerals Corporation proposed mining project in the Cerrillos district, Santa Fe County: Rocky Mountain Center on Environment Report 7, 55 p.

White, L. A., 1948, Miscellaneous notes on the Keresan Pueblos: Michigan Academy of Science Arts and Letters Papers, v. 32, part IV, p. 365-373.

Winship, G. P., 1896, The Coronado expedition, 1540-1542: Bureau of American Ethnology Annual Report 14, p. 329-613.

Yung, M. B. and McCaffery, R. S., 1903, The ore deposits of the San Pedro district, New Mexico: American Institute of Mining and Metallurgical Engineers Transactions, v. 33, p. 350-362.

Burro Salt Train, Sandoval Street, June 1880. Ben Wittick, courtesy Museum of New Mexico.

THE CERRILLOS MINING AREA*

ALBERT H. SCHROEDER
Cultural Properties Review Committee
1108 Barcelona Lane
Santa Fe, New Mexico 87501

INTRODUCTION

The Cerrillos area has a long history of use by man. The nearest Indian pueblos in prehistoric times were San Marcos and San Lázaro (fig. 1), both of which were abandoned in 1680 at the time of the Pueblo Revolt (Schroeder and Matson, 1965). Considerable use of the mineral deposits in the Cerrillos district was made by Indians in prehistoric and early historic times, by Spaniards during the Spanish and Mexican periods, and by U.S. citizens in the American period.

Fragments of Indian pottery at various types of mining sites in the area date from A.D. 900 to 1700 at Indian sites and into the middle 1700s at Spanish sites. The pottery types prior to 1700 as far back as 1300 are decorated with lead-glaze paint. Before and after this period, glaze paint was not used (Snow, 1973; Warren, 1974). It was for use in this decorative treatment between 1300 and 1700 that the Indians mined lead. Pottery associated with the Indian turquoise mines of this area dates prior to 1700 (Snow, 1973).

As a result of the petrographic studies by A. H. Warren, the locales of the manufacture of various pottery types have been identified on the basis of the tempering material used in making the vessels. In turn, the pottery fragments at a mining site indicate which Pueblo people worked the mines since no pottery was made at the mines and the pottery had to be carried in. Pottery most common in the mining sites in the Cerrillos area is a type manufactured at San Marcos Pueblo (Snow, 1973). Indian tools are not present at mines worked by the Spaniards, but non-glaze-decorated Indian pottery, which the Spaniards traded from the Indians, is present at Spanish mines (Warren, 1974).

SPANISH PERIOD

The region of San Marcos Pueblo proved to be of more than ordinary interest to the Spanish explorers. This pueblo, occupied from the 1400s to 1680, is referred to by the Tewa Indians north of Santa Fe as "Turquoise Pueblo Ruin." Nearby Mt. Chalchihuitl (about 3.2 km away), one of the locales of large Indian turquoise workings, the Tewas call "Place of Turquoise." The Cochitis call it "Turquoise Mountain Place" (Harrington, 1916).

The first reference to San Marcos Pueblo occurs in the documents of the Rodriguez-Chamuscado expedition of 1581, naming it Malpartida (unfortunate parting). The report of the venture noted mineral deposits at a site they named San Mateo, located one league (4.2 km) away from the Pueblo (Hammond and Rey, 1927). Lead, turquoise and other mineral deposits occur at this distance from San Marcos.

In 1583, the Espejo expedition left Catiete Pueblo (San Felipe-Katishya) and went to the Pueblo of Santa Catalina which historians mistakenly have thought to be another name applied to both the pueblo and the mineral deposits near San Marcos (Hammond and Rey, 1929). The site was on the north end of the Sandia Mountains.

Eight years later, Castaño de Sosa departed from Cochiti and went to another pueblo (San Marcos) that spoke the same language (Keres), and the following day, he set out to look for mineral deposits. In the following month, when he revisited this same pueblo, he gave it the name "San Marcos, where the mines have been discovered" (Schroeder and Matson, 1965, p. 155). While Castaño went off to visit other pueblos, most of his party remained at San Marcos for 17 days prospecting, and "many tests were made, which showed silver" (Schroeder and Matson, 1965, p. 157). He then led his group to investigate other discoveries, possibly near Cerrillos, following which he went to Santo Domingo; from here, he set out to check other mineral deposits in some mountains, possibly in the north end of the Sandias.

In 1601, a witness in the Valverde investigation of the Oñate colonizing venture reported that near the pueblo of San Marcos, silver lodes assayed by the smelting process produced four ounces, and that at the Pueblo of El Tuerto (possibly the

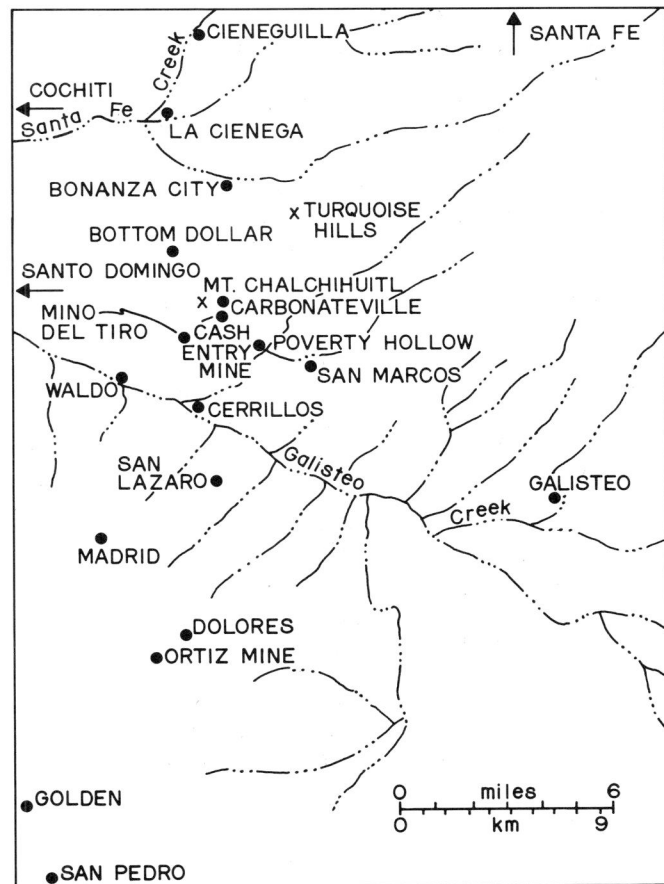

Figure 1. Location map of geographic and cultural features.

---

*Reprinted from LA GACETA, 1977 with permission of El Corral de Santa Fe Westerners.

same as the Santa Catalina of 1583), the sergeant major built machinery to crush and smelt the ore. Between 1598 and 1608, there are many references to minerals near San Marcos (Hammond and Rey, 1953).

In the 1620s, Father Benavides noted that silver and turquoise were found near San Marcos, but that the Indians did not cut the turquoise well (Hodge and others, 1945). Not until 1660 is a Spanish settlement recorded in the area, specifically a farm called Los Cerrillos about two leagues (8.4 km) from San Marcos (Hackett, 1937). This settlement was attacked in the revolt of 1680, but the people survived to join Spaniards from Santa Fe on the retreat south to the El Paso area (Hackett and Shelby, 1942).

When Governor Vargas returned to New Mexico in 1692, he reported that the Pueblo of San Marcos was in ruins (Espinosa, 1942; Leonard, 1932). Coincident with the return of the Spaniards, the Indians ceased mining lead, judging from the pottery associated with their mines. The cause may have been the Spanish need for lead to manufacture bullets. Vargas, in 1694, had a scant supply of bullets, and one of his men, Roque Madrid, reported that his father had worked a lead mine near Santa Fe prior to the revolt (Bancroft, 1962). Vargas sent him with a party to the Cerro de San Marcos where the mine was located. On arrival, they found the shaft filled with earth. Samples showed signs of lead (Espinosa, 1942). As late as 1818, the Spanish need for lead was still evident. A request was sent to various officials, ordering the extraction of lead from the locality named Las Huertas, near or at Placitas, "because of the usual scarcity of that item for bullets" (Twitchell, 1914, vol. I, item 1150).

Spanish use of the Cerrillos region prior to 1680 is noted in contempoary documents. In addition to the farm settlement previously noted, Geronimo de Carvajal, in 1661, is reported as living at Nuestra Señora de los Remedios de los Cerrillos in the jurisdiction of San Marcos Pueblo (Chávez, 1954). A grant in 1692 to Alonzo Rael de Aguila in the same general area shows occupation of a tract that was called Cerrillos prior to the revolt, described as being 4 to 5 leagues (16.8 to 21 km) south of Santa Fe. In 1788, this grant was in the process of being reaffirmed (Twitchell, 1914).

In 1695, an *alcalde* was appointed for a proposed silver mining camp at Cerro de San Marcos. It was established the next year at the former settlement of Los Cerrillos. Vargas reported that he was working three mines there, one showing silver (Espinosa, 1942). In 1709, the Santa Rosa mine in Los Cerrillos of San Marcos, previously owned by Pedro Rodriguez Cubero, was registered. In the following year, another mine, named San Miguel, 15 to 16 leagues (63-67 km) south of Santa Fe, was registered. In 1717, a grant of a lead mine is mentioned as being five leagues (21 km) from Santa Fe, between Cienega and La Cieneguilla, which Twitchell (1914) places near the former town of Bonanza, occupied in the late 1800s.

In 1763, a cross-shaped vein of ore on the south of the hill called "Chalchiquite," named Nuestra Señora de los Dolores, was given as a grant, as was another mine of the same name about one league south of the Cerrillos Ranch in the following year. In 1800, there was a grant for land known as the San Pedro Tract, which is in the present San Pedro area (Twitchell, 1914), as indicated in a petition of 1840.

MEXICAN PERIOD

Gold-bearing rocks were discovered in 1828 on grant land referred to as being on the Santa Rosalia grant or Jose Francisco Ortiz grant (Christiansen, 1974; Jenkinson and Kernberger, 1967; Twitchell, 1914). The rush that followed led to the founding of Dolores near the northeast base of Ortiz Mountain, 1.6 km from which Thomas Edison set up a field laboratory in hopes of developing an electrostatic process to separate the gold from the gravels (Jenkinson and Kernberger, 1967). The area became known as the Old Placer.

Several lodes were located, the most famous being the Ortiz mine in the Ortiz Mountains. The Ortiz grant included the Old Placer district and Dolores (Christiansen, 1974). Most work on the claims took place when melted snow provided the water needed to wash out the gold (Jenkinson and Kernberger, 1967). By 1846, the district was nearly played out. The Ortiz mine, which continued to operate, was sold in 1864 to the New Mexico Mining Company (Christiansen, 1974).

In 1839, another gold rush started in the San Pedro Mountains. The area became known as the New Placer, and the mining camp of Tuerto, 1.6 km northeast of the gold field, became its center. By 1880, the San Pedro and Cañon del Agua Company took over most of the New Placers (Christiansen, 1974; Jenkinson and Kernberger, 1967; Jones, 1904). The above activities also led to the import of some coal from Madrid as early as 1835 to fuel the furnaces. This community, after providing fuel to the railroads for a number of years, began turning into a ghost town in 1949 (Christiansen, 1974; Jenkinson and Kernberger, 1967).

AMERICAN PERIOD

Not until the Mining Act of July 26, 1866, was the land of this region opened to exploration and occupation by U.S. citizens. This was followed by the Placer Mining Act of July 9, 1870, amended May 10, 1872, to provide for the survey and sale of placer lands. The first coal legislation of July 1, 1864 provided for sale by proclamation of the president and was amended March 3, 1865 so that citizens could enter claims for 64 hectares or less (Westphall, 1965).

Mining activities of the Mexican period continued into the American period, particularly in the Old and New Placer regions (Christiansen, 1974; Meline, 1966). In the 1860s, there were exaggerated claims concerning the richness of the mines of New Mexico through artful treatments of legend and optimism which drew some capital to the Cerrillos region. A few companies were successful, though mining was minimal up to 1879 in the Cerrillos area when a lead and silver mining boom got underway and a mining district was formed (Christiansen, 1974; Hayward, 1880), based on codes previously established in California. In 1880, about 100 lodes were being worked (Christiansen, 1974).

In 1879, a group of miners set up Dimick's Camp, later called Turquoise City. Other camps were Purdens Camp, Poverty Hollow, Bonanza City, Carbonateville and Cerrillos Station (Christiansen, 1974; Hayward, 1880). A gold strike this same year, south of Tuerto, led to the birth of Golden (Christiansen, 1974).

The early propaganda on New Mexico's mineral wealth attracted capital to the Cerrillos boom area. Development at some mines was considerable (e.g., a 20.8 km pipeline to bring water to the placers at Golden in 1879), but these ventures often proved unprofitable (Christiansen, 1974). In the 1880s, smelters were being built in Cerrillos. Carbonateville and Bonanza City showed signs of increasing economic gain (New Mexican, April 23, 1882). Coal production increased with the advent of the railroads in the 1880s (Christiansen, 1974; Jenkinson and Kernberger, 1967).

The Cash Entry mine in the 1880s, considered one of the best, was the major employer of the region. The size of its payroll appears to have been exaggerated (Christiansen, 1974), as do such stories of scraping silver loose in the mine with a butter knife. The operation of the mine reportedly was carried on in complete secrecy (Jenkinson and Kernberger, 1967). Owned by an English company that shipped the ore to Wales, it was sold in the late 1880s when silver values dropped; it has been worked intermittently over the succeeding years (Christiansen, 1974).

The Cash Entry experienced mine jumpers, reported a great strike, received periodic news releases, and had management problems (New Mexican, Jan. 20, 1883; Aug. 12, 1885; Aug. 8, 1890; Oct. 27, 1891). Other newspaper reports cover incidents in the Cerrillos mining district, such as masked men refusing entry on the Mina del Tiro property or the accidental discovery of an old shaft with Indian tools in it, as at the Bottom Dollar (New Mexican, Feb. 14, 1883).

With the decrease in mining values in the district as well as poor returns for several years, Bonanza City and Carbonateville, after 1890, became ghost towns. Turquoise City only lasted briefly. However, Cerrillos and Golden survived as small towns (Christiansen, 1974). Renchan's claim was worked a bit in 1911, but no turquoise was sold, and other turquoise claims lapsed due to lack of assessment work (Sterrett, 1912). After about 1895, there was little demand for turquoise (Hodge and others, 1945), and most of the turquoise mines were closed. Work in the Golden area proved to be unprofitable due to the lack of water (Christiansen, 1974).

Among the propaganda on the richness of the Cerrillos district were statements on the value of the turquoise extracted. Northrop (1959) points out that little trust can be placed in the figures released in New Mexico. In a recent article (Northrop, 1973), he compares Governor Otero's figures for New Mexico's turquoise production and those of the U.S. Geological Survey for U.S. total production for the years 1891 through 1896 (Table 1). The discrepancies are obvious. In 1965, the directory of mines shows the Cash Entry O/Pit as one of the few still active, producing gold, silver and copper (File, 1965).

INDIAN USE

We have no evidence of Indian use of the turquoise mines in the Cerrillos area after 1700 throughout the remainder of the Spanish and Mexican periods. In the American period, the mines were reported first in 1858, when W. P. Blake described the ancient workings at Mt. Chalchihuitl (Jones, 1904). Pogue (1915, p. 52-53), who produced a detailed monograph on the subject of turquoise, quotes from Blake and other early visitors to Mt. Chalchihuitl who stated that there had been "extensive prehistoric mining operations" here and that at the bottom of the workings "pine trees over a hundred years old are now growing" (in 1858), and that "on the slopes and sides of the great piles of rubbish are growing large cedars and pines, the age of which . . . must be reckoned in centuries" (in 1881). "Ancient" excavations that exceeded the size of recent excavations also were found at other modern worked locales and several places on Turquoise Hill. He concluded that the "immense excavations at Cerrillos are of great antiquity."

These "ancient" turquoise workings evidently had been rather complete in removing good material, as indicated by the considerable exploratory work undertaken at Mt. Chalchihuitl by J. B. Hyde in 1880, which "proved unsuccessful" (Pogue, 1915, p. 53). The estimated age of the trees growing in the mines and dumps coincides closely with the conclusion of the archaeologists that various turquoise mines in the Cerrillos district were abandoned at about 1700 (Snow, 1973; Warren, 1974).

The activities of Pueblo Indians at turquoise workings in the Cerrillos area in the American period were not major efforts. In 1858, it was reported that two or three Indians came to Mt. Chalchihuitl to search the surface for turquoise (Pogue, 1915). In 1866, Meline (1966, p. 178) referred to the Cerrillos Turquoise mine and stated "it is said that numerous moccasin tracks in the neighborhood of the mine show that it is frequently visited by them at night." In 1881, Bandelier met two Indians working in an old shaft at Cerrillos, cutting out turquoise with hatchets (Lange and Riley, 1966).

It would seem that the material the Indians were able to obtain in the early American period was inferior turquoise. Bourke reported in 1881 that young men from Santo Domingo boarded the train to sell specimens of turquoise. "It is not genuine turquoise, but rather an impure malachite (Bloom, 1936, p. 78). Jones (1904) remarked that perhaps much of the supposed turquoise used by Pueblos was malachite, the latter being common in ancient graves associated with turquoise. He also noted that at both Chalchihuitl and Turquesa (Turquoise Hills) turquoise is much altered by kaolinization.

Sterrett (1912, p. 1070-1071) remarked that "Indians still obtain turquoise either from localities known only to themselves or from well-known mines either not now in operation or under guard." He also stated that in New Mexico in 1918, "probably not over 10 or 15 pounds was the best selected pure gem" and that little pure turquoise has been recovered since the last regular mining a number of years ago. Prior to the 1920s, the Santo Domingos only brought raw turquoise in the matrix to the Zunis. After the turquoise mines in Colorado and Nevada opened up in the 1920s and the stones became more plentiful, the Santo Domingos were able to bring finished turquoise beads to the Zunis (Adair, 1944).

The lack of any mention of Indians mining turquoise from the 1700s on, along with the latest dated pottery at Indian mines being 1700, strongly suggests a cessation of Indian activity by this date. In addition, the estimated age of trees growing in the mines in 1858 as being more than 100 years old, and the lack of any reference to Indian mining in the American period further support a lack of such activity. Aside

Table 1. Turquoise Production According to Two Sources (from Northrop, 1973).

Year	U.S.G.S. (for U.S.)	Gov. Otero (for N.M.)
1891	$150,000	$150,000
1892	175,000	175,000
1893	143,000	200,000
1894	34,000	250,000
1895	50,000	350,000
1896	40,000	475,000

from searching of the surface of old mines or entering mines opened or reopened during the American period by U.S. miners, the Rio Grande Pueblo Indians probably did not mine turquoise in the Cerrillos area after 1700, or if they did, it was on a very minor scale and infrequent.

SUMMARY

The Cerrillos area has had a rather unique tricultural mining history from prehistoric times to the present, involving extraction of lead, turquoise, silver, copper and gold along with minor amounts of other minerals. The local economies of each cultural group required some of these minerals at one period or another for one purpose or another. As the local supply of ores diminished, the mining sites were abandoned, thus forcing the people to look elsewhere to fill their needs, and if unsuccessful, to discontinue locally the practice or art associated with the mineral involved. The Cerrillos area has been exploited by the Indians for approximately 400 years (1300-1700), by the Spaniards and Mexicans for more than 200 years (1598-1840s), and by U.S. miners for about 100 years. The state of New Mexico has recognized the significance of this historical area, and in February 1973, placed the "Cerrillos Mining District" on the State Register of Cultural Properties and recommended it to the National Register of Historic Places.

REFERENCES

Adair, J., 1944, The Navajo and Pueblo silversmiths: University of Oklahoma Press, Norman, 220 p.

Bancroft, H. H., 1962, History of Arizona and New Mexico, 1530-1888: Horn and Wallace, Albuquerque, 829 p.

Bloom, L., ed., 1935-36, Bourke on the Southwest: New Mexico Historical Review, v. 10, p. 271-322; v. 11, p. 77-122.

Chávez, A., 1954, Origins of New Mexico families: Historical Society of New Mexico, Santa Fe, 339 p.

Christiansen, P. W., 1974, The story of mining in New Mexico: New Mexico Bureau of Mines and Mineral Resources Scenic Trips to the Geologic Past 12, 112 p.

Espinosa, J. M., 1942, Crusaders of the Rio Grande: Institute of Jesuit History, Chicago, 410 p.

File, L. A., 1965, Directory of mines of New Mexico: New Mexico Bureau of Mines and Mineral Resources Circular 77, 188 p.

Hackett, C. W., 1937, Historical documents relating to New Mexico, Nueva Vizcaya, and approaches thereto, to 1773: Carnegie Institution of Washington, Washington, 532 p.

Hackett, C. W. and Shelby, C. C., 1942, Revolt of the Pueblo Indians of New Mexico and Otermin's attempted reconquest, 1680-1682, v. 8: University of New Mexico Press, Albuquerque, 262 p.

Hammond, G. P. and Rey, A., 1927, The Gallegos relation of the Rodriguez-Chamuscado expedition to New Mexico: Historical Society of New Mexico Publications in History, v. 4, 69 p.

————, 1929, Expedition into New Mexico made by Antonio de Espejo, 1582-1583, as revealed in the journal of Diego Pérez de Luxán: The Quivira Society, Los Angeles, 143 p.

————, 1953, Don Juan de Oñate, colonizer of New Mexico, 1595-1628, v. 5-6: University of New Mexico Press, Albuquerque, 1187 p.

Harrington, J. P., 1916, The ethnogeography of the Tewa Indians: Bureau of American Ethnology Annual Report 29, 636 p.

Hayward, J. L., 1880, The Los Cerrillos mines and their mineral resources . . . accompanied by a map of the same, drawn from actual surveys: J. C. Clark Printing Co., South Framingham, 98 p.

Hodge, F. W., Hammond, G. P. and Rey, A., 1945, Fray Alonso de Benavides' revised memorial of 1634: University of New Mexico Press, Albuquerque, 368 p.

Jenkinson, M. and Kernberger, K., 1967, Ghost towns of New Mexico: University of New Mexico Press, Albuquerque, 156 p.

Jones, F. A., 1904, New Mexico mines and minerals: The New Mexican Printing Company, Santa Fe, 214 p.

Lange, C. H. and Riley, C. L., 1966, The Southwestern journals of Adolph F. Bandelier, 1880-1882: University of New Mexico Press, The School of American Research, and the Museum of New Mexico Press, Albuquerque and Santa Fe, 462 p.

Leonard, I. A., 1932, The Mercurio Volante of Don Carlos de Sigüenza y Góngora, an account of the first expedition of Don Diego de Vargas into New Mexico in 1692: The Quivira Society, Los Angeles, 136 p.

Meline, F., 1966, Two thousand miles on horseback, Santa Fé and back: Horn and Wallace, Albuquerque, 317 p.

New Mexican, Issues of April 23, 1882; January 20, 1883; February 14, 1883; August 12, 1885; August 8, 1890; October 27, 1891.

Northrop, S. A., 1959, Minerals of New Mexico: University of New Mexico Press, Albuquerque, 665 p.

————, 1973, Turquoise: Museum of New Mexico, Santa Fe, p. 3-22.

Pogue, J. E., 1915, The turquoise: National Academy of Sciences Memoir 12, part II, 162 p.

Schroeder, A. H. and Matson, D. S., 1965, A colony on the move, Gaspar Castaño de Sosa's journal, 1590-1591: School of American Research, Santa Fe, 196 p.

Snow, D. H., 1973, Prehistoric Southwestern turquoise industry, in Turquoise: Museum of New Mexico, Santa Fe, p. 33-47.

Sterrett, D. B., 1912, Gems and precious stones, in Mineral resources of the United States, part II: U.S. Geological Survey, Washington, p. 1066-1071.

Twitchell, R. E., 1914, The Spanish archives of New Mexico, v. 1: The Torch Press, Cedar Rapids, 525 p.

Warren, A. H., 1974, An archaeological survey of the Occidental Minerals Corporation proposed mining project area in the Cerrillos district, Santa Fe County, New Mexico, in Rocky Mountain Center on Environment, 1976, Romcoe environmental study, Oxymin Cerrillos project: Romcoe, Denver, 55 p.

Westphall, V., 1965, The public domain in New Mexico, 1854-1891: University of New Mexico Press, Albuquerque, 212 p.

THE BATTLE OF GLORIETA PASS, 1862

H. L. JAMES*
New Mexico State Highway Department
P.O. Box 1149
Santa Fe, New Mexico 87501

During the latter part of the 19th century, there was located at the present site of Cañoncito a place called Johnson's ranch. The buildings and corrals served as supply base for General Henry H. Sibley's Confederate forces during the Civil War Battle of Glorieta Pass. Referred to by some as "The Gettysburg of The Southwest," the battle occurred on March 26-28, 1862.

Fresh and confident from their decisive victory at Valverde on February 21, and already in occupation of Fort Craig, Albuquerque and Santa Fe, Sibley's "Texas rangers" (fig. 1) now set their sights on Fort Union, their last major obstacle before the ultimate goal, possession of gold fields in the southern Rockies.

With the territorial seat of government now transferred to Las Vegas, the Union forces (First Regiment, Colorado Volunteers) under command of Colonel John P. Slough, chose to surprise the advancing enemy on the road and to recapture the capital city. The "surprise" occurred at 2:00 P.M. on the afternoon of March 26 and was so sudden that the two advance guards literally were startled by the presence of the other. This incident was immediately west of Glorieta summit (fig. 2) where a skirmish line was established across a small valley, and the battle ensued. The first conflict lasted for three hours, during the course of which the Confederates were driven back to a second line of defense at a bridge (whose rock abutments are still in place) over Galisteo Creek. It was here that the first day's battle ended with the Texans withdrawing to Johnson's ranch and the Volunteers regrouping on the east side of the summit at a place called Pigeon's ranch.

The following day, by mutual agreement between the two opposing commanders, hostilities were suspended to care for wounded and to bury the dead. The Union losses were reported as 5 killed, 14 wounded and 3 missing; while the Confederates sustained 30 killed, 40 wounded and 70 captured (Archambeau, 1964).

On the morning of March 28, the Confederates, under the command of Colonel William R. Scurry, began their attack march through the pass, leaving behind a small detachment to guard the supply base. The second battle line was drawn in the clearing just north of Pigeon's ranch, and here in mid-morning commenced the major conflict that was to last the entire day. During the course of the battle, and unknown to the Texans, a significant strategy was being undertaken. Under the leadership of Major John M. Chivington, a detachment of men was sent in a westerly route atop Glorieta Mesa; after an ardous march of 8 miles (13 km), they attacked and completely destroyed the Confederate supply camp at Johnson's ranch (fig. 2).

Meanwhile, back at Pigeon's ranch, another armistice was negotiated in late afternoon, again to remove the wounded and dead. The casualty records for the second battle were: Union dead 48, wounded 65; Confederate dead 36, wounded 60 (Archambeau, 1964).

After darkness, Union troops withdrew from the field to their headquarters south of Pecos ruins to prepare a second line of defense for the following day. The Confederates remained at Pigeon's, sensing the upper hand with their foes seemingly in retreat. But with news of the fatal blow inflicted at Johnson's ranch, the southern cause was dashed and further advance was hopeless.

Now, without food, ammunition, medical supplies, horses and wagons, General Sibley ordered a withdrawal to Albuquerque, where he buried his artillery, and began what he termed his "retrograde movement," but what in reality was a desperate, death-march retreat back to El Paso.

Figure 1. One of Sibley's "Texas rangers." This sketch, copied from an original woodcut, appears in Lossing's Pictorial History of the Civil War, 1868. *The ferocious-looking Confederate is most likely the imagination of a Union artist.*

*Present address: Montana Bureau of Mines and Geology; Butte, Montana 59701.

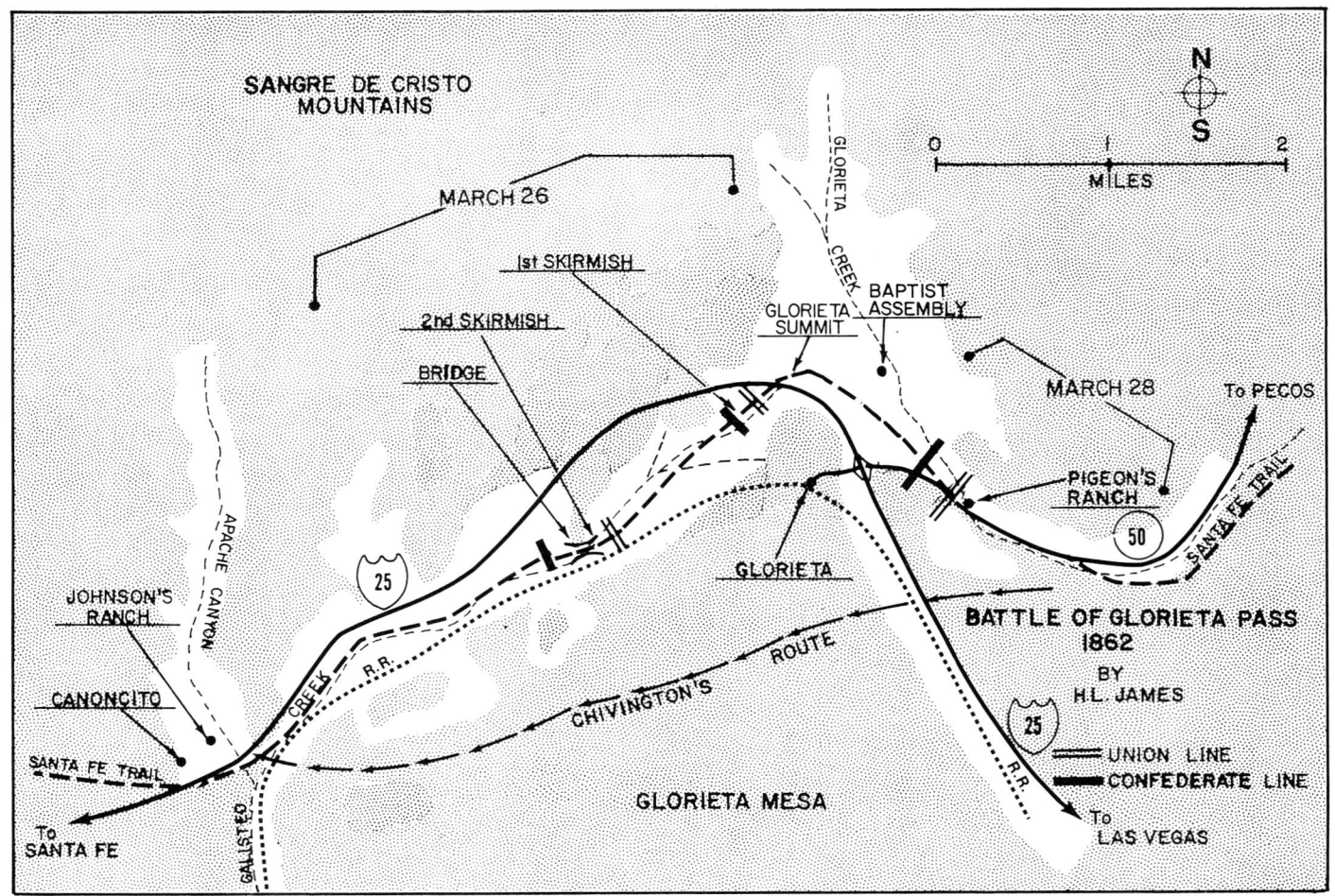

Figure 2. Map of the Battle of Glorieta Pass and present environs.

So ended the Civil War in the Southwest. What with the grand campaigns in the East, the Battle of Glorieta Pass might be classed by most historians as a minor skirmish. But during those three fateful days in March, along a remote canyon in New Mexico, the combined death loss of 119 Americans was just as tragic.

REFERENCE

Archambeau, E. R., Jr., 1964, The New Mexico campaign, 1861-1862: Pandhandle-Plains Historical Review, v. 37, p. 3-32.